D0095735

THE AMERICAN NIGHT

Also by Jim Morrison

WILDERNESS

THE
AMERICAN NIGHT

THE WRITINGS OF
JIM MORRISON
VOLUME II

VINTAGE BOOKS
A DIVISION OF RANDOM HOUSE, INC.
NEW YORK

First Vintage Books Edition, August 1991

Copyright © 1990 by Wilderness Publications
Photographs copyright © 1990 by Frank J. Lisciandro
Song lyrics on pages 39, 40, 41, 42, 43, 44, 45, 49, 50, 51, 52, 97, 98, 101, 102, 105, 106, 107, 109, 110, 111, 112, 113, 114, 115, 116, 125, 126, 127, 156 copyright © Doors Music Co.

All rights reserved under International and Pan-American Copyright Conventions. Published in the United States by Vintage Books, a division of Random House, Inc., New York, and simultaneously in Canada by Random House of Canada Limited, Toronto. Originally published in hardcover by Villard Books, a division of Random House, Inc., New York, in 1990.

Library of Congress Cataloging-in-Publication Data
Morrison, Jim, 1943-1971.
  The American night.—1st Vintage Books ed.
    p.   cm.—(The lost writings of Jim Morrison ; v. 2)
  Includes index.
  ISBN 0-679-73462-7 (pbk.)
    I. Title.   II. Series: Morrison, Jim, 1943-1971. Lost writings of Jim Morrison (Vintage Books (Firm)) ; v. 2.
  PS3563.08746A84   1991
  811'.54—dc20   90-50901
                          CIP

Manufactured in the United States of America
10 9 8 7 6 5 4 3 2 1

OPEN

The Night is young
          & full of rest
I can't describe the
          way she's dress'd
She'll pander to some strange
          requests
Anything that you suggest
Anything to please her guest

(from *WILDERNESS*)

for
Pamela Susan

CONTENTS

AN AMERICAN PRAYER

Do you Know the warm progress
                    under the stars ?
Do you Know we exist ?
Have you forgotten the keys to the Kingdom ?
Have you been borne yet
                    & are you alive ?

Let's reinvent the gods, all the myths
                                        of the ages
Celebrate symbols from deep elder forests
[Have you forgotten the lessons
                    of the ancient war]

We need great golden copulations

The fathers are cackling in trees of the forest
Our mother is dead in sea

Do you know we are being led to
          slaughters by placid admirals
& that fat slow generals are getting
    obscene on young blood

Do you know the warm progress
                        under the stars?
Do you know we exist?
Have you forgotten the keys
            to the Kingdom?
Have you been borne yet
                        & are you alive?

Let's reinvent the gods, all the myths
                            of the ages
Celebrate symbols from deep elder forests
[Have you forgotten the lessons
                        of the ancient war]

We need great golden copulations

The fathers are cackling in trees of the forest
Our mother is dead in the sea

Do you know we are being led to
            slaughters by placid admirals
& that fat slow generals are getting
            obscene on young blood

Do you know we are ruled by T. V.
The moon is a dry blood beast
Guerrilla bands are rolling numbers
    in the next block of green vine
amassing for warfare on innocent herdsmen
    who are just dying

O great creator of being
grant us one more hour to
    perform our art
    & perfect our lives

The moths & atheists are doubly divine
    & dying
We live, we die
& death not ends it
Journey we more into the
    Nightmare
Cling to life
    our passion'd flower
Cling to cunts & cocks
    of despair
We got our final vision
    by clap
Columbus' groin got
    filled w/green death

(I touched her thigh
    & death smiled)

We have assembled inside this ancient
  & insane theatre
To propagate our lust for life
  & flee the swarming wisdom
      of the streets
The barns are stormed
The windows kept
& only one of all the rest
To dance & save us
W/the divine mockery
  of words
Music inflames temperament

  (When the true King's murderers
   are allowed to roam free
   a 1000 Magicians arise
    in the land)

Where are the feasts
  we were promised
Where is the wine
  The New Wine
    (dying on the vine)

resident mockery
give us an hour for magic
We of the purple glove
We of the starling flight
& velvet hour
We of arabic pleasure's breed
We of sundome & the night

Give us a creed
To believe
A night of Lust
Give us trust in
The Night

Give of color
hundred hues
a rich Mandala
for me & you

& for your silky
pillowed house
a head, wisdom
& a bed

Troubled decree
Resident mockery
has claimed thee

We used to believe
in the good old days
We still receive
In little ways

The Things of Kindness
& unsporting brow
Forget & allow

Did you know freedom exists
    in a school book
Did you know madmen are
    running our prison
w/in a jail, w/in a gaol
w/in a white free protestant
Maelstrom

We're perched headlong
    on the edge of boredom
We're reaching for death
    on the end of a candle
We're trying for something
    That's already found us

We can invent Kingdoms of our own
grand purple thrones, those chairs of lust
& love we must, in beds of rust

Steel doors lock in prisoner's screams
& muzak, AM, rocks their dreams
No black men's pride to hoist the beams
while mocking angels sift what seems

To be a collage of magazine dust
Scratched on foreheads of walls of trust
This is just jail for those who must
get up in the morning & fight for such

unusable standards
while weeping maidens
show-off penury & pout
ravings for a mad
staff

Wow, I'm sick of doubt
Live in the light of certain
South

Cruel bindings
The servants have the power
dog-men & their mean women
pulling poor blankets over
our sailors
(& where were you in our
    lean hour)
Milking your moustache?
or grinding a flower?
I'm sick of dour faces
Staring at me from the T.V.
Tower. I want roses in
my garden bower;   dig?
Royal babies, rubies
must now replace aborted
Strangers in the mud
These mutants, blood-meal
for the plant that's plowed

They are waiting to take us into
                  the severed garden
Do you know how pale & wanton thrillful
        comes death on a strange hour
        unannounced, unplanned for
like a scaring over-friendly guest you've
        brought to bed
Death makes angels of us all
        & gives us wings
where we had shoulders
        smooth as raven's
           claws

No more money, no more fancy dress
This other Kingdom seems by far the best
until its other jaw reveals incest
& loose obedience to a vegetable law

I will not go
Prefer a Feast of Friends
To the Giant family

❖

II

Great screaming Christ
Upsy-daisy
Lazy Mary will you get up
upon a Sunday morning

"The movie will begin in 5 moments"
The mindless Voice announced
"All those unseated, will await
The next show"

We filed slowly, languidly
into the hall. The auditorium
was vast, & silent.
As we seated & were darkened
The Voice continued:

"The program for this evening
is not new. You have seen
This entertainment thru & thru.
You've seen your birth, your
life & death; you might recall
all of the rest—(did you
have a good world when you
died?)—enough to base
a movie on?"

An iron chuckle rapped our
minds like a fist.

I'm getting out of here
Where're you going?
To the other side of morning
Please don't chase the clouds
pagodas, temples

Her cunt gripped him
like a warm friendly
hand.

"It's all right.
All your friends are here."

When can I meet them?
"After you've eaten"
I'm not hungry
"O, we meant beaten"

Silver stream, silvery scream,
impossible concentration

Here come the comedians
look at them smile
Watch them dance
an indian mile

Look at them gesture
How aplomb
So to gesture everyone

Words dissemble
Words be quick
Words resemble walking sticks

Plant them
They will grow
Watch them waver so

I'll always be
a word-man
Better than a birdman

But I'll charge
Won't get away
w/out lodging a dollar

Shall I say it again
aloud, you get the point
No food w/out fuel's gain

I'll be, the irish loud
unleashed my beak
at peak of powers

O girl, unleash
your worried comb

O worried mind

Sin in the fallen
Backwoods by the blind

She smells debt
on my new collar

Arrogant prose
Tied in a network of fast quest
Hence the obsession

Its quick to admit
Fast borrowed rhythm
Woman came between them

Women of the world unite
Make the world safe
For a scandalous life

Hee Heee
Cut your throat
Life is a joke

Your wife's in a moat
The same boat
Here comes the goat

Blood Blood Blood Blood
They're making a joke
of our universe

❖

III

Matchbox
Are you more real than me
I'll burn you, & set you free
Wept bitter tears
Excessive courtesy
I won't forget

❖

IV

A hot sick lava flowed up,
Rustling & bubbling.
The paper face.
Mirror-mask, I love you mirror.

He had been brainwashed for 4 hrs.
The LT. puzzled in again
    "ready to talk"
"No sir"—was all he'd say.
        Go back to the gym.
        Very peaceful
        Meditation

Air base in the desert
looking out venetian blinds
a plane
a desert flower
cool cartoon

The rest of the World
is reckless & dangerous
Look at the
brothels
Stag films
Exploration

❖

V

A ship leaves port
mean horse of another thicket
wishbone of desire
decry the metal fox

❖

❖

Poems from
TAPE NOON

JIM MORRISON

*We must tie all these
desperate impressions together*

MONEY...

Money, the beauty of

> (currency
> pale grccn
> greasy
> ornate
> soft
> furrowed
> texture)

Skin or leather

❖

ENTER THE SLIP

Enter the slip
of the warm womb tide

Wet labyrinth kiss

digging the wells
& riding the lies

all holes & poles

Walk down a street
A drive to the beach
Drowning man's flash
A town in siege

❖

THE DESERT

The Desert
—roseate metallic blue
& insect green

blank mirrors &
pools of silver

a universe in
one body

BIBULOUS COMPOUND OF

Bibulous compound of
    muck & mulch milk

Tenebrous connections
    in forest & farm

all-swarming dish-like
    elegance

    Say No More

—That sure was a mouthful.
—You said it.

❖

YOU MUST CONFRONT

you must confront
    your life
which is sneaking up
    on you
like a rapt coiled
    serpent

snail–slime

you must confront
      the inevitable
        eventually
Bloody Bones has got you!

❖

HOPE IS JUST...

hope is just a word
    when you think in
            Table Cloths
Laughter will not end
    her funny feeling
    or assuage our
          strange desire
Children will be born

❖

WELCOME TO THE AMERICAN NIGHT

Welcome to the American Night
where dogs bite
to find the voice
        the face the fate the fame
to be tamed
        by The Night
in a quiet soft luxuriant
                        car
Hitchhikers line the Great Highway

❖

COCK-PIT

Cock-pit
I am real
   Take a snapshot of me
He is real, shot
Reality is what has been
      concealed from us
        for so long
birth sex death
we're alive when we laugh
when we can feel the
    rush & spurt of blood
blood is real in its redness
the rainbow is real in
    absence of blood

❖

SUDDEN ATTACK

Sudden attack
Stabbed & hacked but no
pain   no   death

Zone of silence
Sudden powered
        mute strangeness
                & awareness
        most awkward to the mind
                alive w/love & laughter
        & memory sweet of kinder
                times
        when we spoke & words
                had soft form by
                        a fire

❖

THIS IS MY FOREST

This is my forest
    a sea of wires.
This gaggle of vision
    is my flame.
These trees are men,
    the engineers.
And a tribe of farmers
    on their Sunday off.

Gods—the directors.
    Cameras, greek
Centaurs on the boom,
    sliding w/silent
Mobile grace

Toward me—
    a leaping clown
In the great sun's
    eye.

Grand danger there
    in curved thigh.
The avenging finger—
    lord.

❖

DANCING & THRASHING

Dancing & thrashing
    the reptile summer
They'll be here long
    before we're gone
Sunning themselves
    on the marble porch
Raging w/in against
    the slow heat
Of an invaded Town

The Kingdom is ours

❖

TRANSLATIONS OF THE DIVINE

Translations of the divine
in all languages. The Blues,
The records get you high,
in armies / on swift channels.
The new dreamer will sing
to the mind w/thoughts
unclutched by speech.
Pirate mind stations. Las Vegas T.V.
Midnite showings.

❖

ELECTRIC STORM

electric storm
  from the front
barometer at zero
  forest
blue-eyed dog
  strangled by snow
Night storm
  flight-drive thru deserts
neon capitals, Wilderness
  echoed & silenced
   by angels

Angel Flight
 to tobacco farm
the roadhouse
 tomorrow

get ready for the Night
 the rumors on waking
a gradual feeling of
 learning & remembering

imagine a heaven in the
 night-time
  would one member be missing?

❖

THE FORM IS AN ANGEL...

The form is an angel of soul
    from horse to man to boy
      & back again

Music sex & idea are the
    currents of connection

friendship transition

conductor of soul from the
    fat brain of stealth
      to sunset

Work out

Welcome to the night
Welcome to the deep good
    dark American Night

a man gets time to die
    his amber waste

sloven footsteps of swine

in the camps, w/dark black
                lumber
crooked stars have destiny's
                number

Lord help us

❖

LEAVE THE INFORMED SENSE

Leave the informed sense
in our wake
you be Christ
on this package tour
—Money beats soul—

Last words, last words
out

❖

CELEBRATION OF
THE LIZARD

Lions in the street & roaming
Dogs in heat, rabid, foaming
A beast caged in the heart of a city

The body of his mother
Rotting in the summer ground.
He fled the town.

He went down South
And crossed the border
Left the chaos & disorder
Back there
Over his shoulder.

One morning he awoke in a green hotel
W/a strange creature groaning beside him.
Sweat oozed from its shiny skin.

Is everybody in? (3)
The ceremony is about to begin.

Wake up!
You can't remember where it was.
Had this dream stopped?
The snake was pale gold glazed & shrunken.
We were afraid to touch it.
The sheets were hot dead prisons.
And she was beside me, old,
She's, no; young.
Her dark red hair.
The white soft skin.
Now, run to the mirror in the bathroom,
Look!
She's coming in here.
I can't live thru each slow century
   of her moving.
I let my cheek slide down
The cool smooth tile
Feel the good cold stinging blood.
The smooth hissing snakes
   of rain . . .

Once I had, a little game
I liked to crawl, back into my brain
I think you know, the game I mean
I mean the game, called 'go insane'

Now you should try, this little game
Just close your eyes, forget your name
forget the world, forget the people
and we'll erect, a different steeple.

This little game, is fun to do.
Just close your eyes, no way to lose
And I'm right there, I'm going too
Release control, we're breaking Thru

Burrow back into the brain
Way back past the realm of pain
Back where there's never any rain

And the rain falls gently on the town.
And over the heads of all of us
And in the labyrinth of streams
Beneath, the quiet unearthly presence of
Nervous hill dwellers in the gentle hills around,
Reptiles abounding
Fossils, caves, cool air heights.

(Each house repeats a mold,
      Windows rolled, beast car
           locked in against morning.

All now sleeping, rugs silent,
      Mirrors vacant, dust blind
          under the beds

Of lawful couples wound
      in sheets & daughters,
          smug w/semen, eyes
              in their nipples.)

Wait!

There's been a slaughter here.
      (siren)

      (Don't stop to speak or look around
      Your gloves & fan are on the ground
      We're getting out of town
      We're going on the run
      And you're the one I want to come)

Not to touch the earth
Not to see the sun
Nothing left to do,
But run, run, run
Let's run

House upon the hill
Moon is lying still
Shadows of the trees
Witnessing the wild breeze
C'mon baby
Run w/me
Let's run

The mansion is warm at the top of the hill
Rich are the rooms & the comforts there
Red are the arms of luxuriant chairs
& you won't know a thing till you get inside.

Dead president's corpse in the driver's car
The engine runs on glue and tar
C'mon along, we're not going very far
To the East to meet the Czar.

Some outlaws lived by the side of a lake
The minister's daughter's in love w/the snake
Who lives in a well by the side of the road
Wake up, girl, we're almost home.

Sun Sun Sun
Burn Burn Burn
Soon Soon Soon

Moon-Moon-Moon
I will get you
Soon
Soon
Soon!

(Scream)

Let the carnival bells ring
Let the serpent sing
Let everything

(Bells)

Fade
Desert Night
Voices of the Fire

"We came down the rivers & highways
We came down from forests & falls
We came down from Carson & Springfield
We came down from Phoenix enthralled

And I can tell you the names of the Kingdom
I can tell you the things that you know
Listening for a fistful of silence
Climbing valleys into the shade"

Sounds of the Fire
(whistles, rattlesnakes, castanets)

"I am the Lizard King
I can do anything
I can make the earth stop in its tracks
I made the blue cars go away.

For seven years I dwelt
in the loose palace of exile,
Playing strange games
w/the girls of the island.

Now I have come again
To the land of the fair, & the strong, & the wise.

Brothers & sisters of the pale forest
O Children of Night
Who among you will run w/the hunt?

—Cries of assent—

Now Night arrives with her purple legion.
Retire now to your tents & to your dreams.
Tomorrow we enter the town of my birth.
I want to be ready."

|

Music
— Fade —
end

|

❖

Music by The Doors
Copyright © 1970, Doors Music Co.

◆

THE SOFT PARADE

When I was back there in seminary school
There was a person there
Who put forth the proposition
That you can petition the Lord with prayer
Petition the Lord with prayer
Petition the Lord with prayer
You cannot petition the Lord with prayer!

Can you give me sanctuary
I must find a place to hide
A place for me to hide

Can you find me soft asylum
I can't make it any more
The Man is at the door

Peppermint, miniskirts, chocolate candy
Champion sax & a girl named Sandy
There's only 4 ways to get unraveled
One is to sleep & the other is travel
One is a bandit up in the hills
& one is to love your neighbor till
his wife gets home

Catacombs
Nursery bones
Winter women
growing stones
Carrying babies
to the river

Streets & shoes
Avenues
Leather riders
selling news
The Monk Bought Lunch

Successful hills are here to stay
Everything must be this way
gentle street where people play
Welcome to the soft parade

All our lives we sweat & save
Building for a shallow grave
There must be something else we say
Somehow to defend this place
(Everything must be this way)

The soft parade has now begun
Listen to the engines hum
People out to have some fun
A cobra on my left
                a leopard on my right

The deer woman in a silk dress
Girls w/beads around their necks
Kiss the hunter of the green vest
Who has wrestled before
              w/lions in the night

Out of sight!
The lights are getting brighter
The radio is moaning
Calling to the dogs
There are still a few animals
        left out in the yard
But it's getting harder
        to describe sailors
                to the underfed

Tropic corridor
Tropic treasure
What got us this far
To this mild equator?

We need someone or something new
Something else to get us thru

Calling on the dogs
Calling on the dogs
Calling on the dogs
Calling in the dogs
Calling all the dogs
Calling on the gods

Meet me
At the crossroads
Meet me
At the edge of town
Outskirts of the city
Just you & I
& the evening sky
You'd better come alone
You'd better bring your gun
We're gonna have some fun!

When all else fails
      We can whip the horse's
      eyes & make them sleep
      & cry

❖

Words and Music by Jim Morrison
Copyright © 1969, Doors Music Co.

❖

Poems from
THE VILLAGE READING

IN THAT YEAR...

In that year we had a great visitation of energy.

Back in those days everything
was simpler & more confused.
One summer night, going
To the pier, I ran into
2 young girls. The
blonde was called Freedom,
the dark one, Enterprise.
We talked, & they told
me this story.

❖

& THE COOL FLUTTERING...

    & the cool fluttering rotten wind
    & a child's hand-print on
       picture window
    & the guncocked held
       on the shoulder.
    & fire in the night
       waiting, in a darkened house
       for the cruel insane breed
       from town to arrive
       & come poking thru smoke
       & the fuel & ashes for milk
       & the evil leer on their faces
         barking w/triumph
Who will not stop them?
The hollow tree, where
       we three slept & dreamed
       in the movement of
       whirling shadows & grass
Tired rustle of leaves
An oldman stirs the dancers
       w/his old dance
    darkening
swift shadows lean on the
       meat of forests
       to allow breathing

& THE COOL FLUTTERING...

    Gently they stir
    Gently rise
    The dead are new-born
      awakening
    w/ravaged limbs
    & wet souls
    Gently they sigh
      in rapt funeral amazement
    Who called these dead to dance?
    Was it the young woman
      learning to play the "Ghost
      Song" on her baby grand
    Was it the wilderness children?
      Was it the Ghost-God himself,
      stuttering, cheering,
      chatting blindly?
        ——I called you up to
          anoint the earth.
          I called you to announce
          sadness falling like
          burned skin
          I called you to wish
          you well, to glory in
          self like a new monster
          & now I call on you
          to pray:

❖

Lament for my cock
Sore & crucified
I seek to know you
acquiring soulful wisdom
you can open walls of
mystery
strip-show

How to ~~acquire~~ get death
On the morning
show

T.V. death
which the child
absorbs

death-well
mystery
which makes
me write

Slow train
The death of my cock
gives life

Forgive the poor old people
who gave us entry
Taught us God
& the child's prayer
in the night

Guitar player
Ancient wise satyr
Sing your ode
to my cock
caress its lament
stiffen & guide
us
~~we frozen~~

LAMENT FOR THE DEATH OF MY COCK

Lament for my cock
Sore & crucified
I seek to know you
acquiring soulful wisdom
you can open walls of
mystery
strip-show

How to get death
On the morning
show

T.V. death
which the child
absorbs

death-well
mystery
which makes
me write

Slow train
The death of my cock
gives life

Guitar player
Ancient wise satyr
Sing your ode
to my cock
caress its lament
stiffen & guide
us

LAMENT FOR THE DEATH OF MY COCK

Lost cells
The knowledge of cancer
To speak to the heart
& give the great gift
words

power

trance

This stable friend
& the beasts of his zoo
wild, haired chicks
each color connects
to create the boat
which rocks the race

could any hell be more
horrible than now
& real

"I pressed her thigh
& death smiled"

death, old friend
death & my cock
are the world

LAMENT FOR THE DEATH OF MY COCK

I can forgive
my injuries
in the name of
wisdom

luxury

romance

Sentence upon sentence.
Words are healing.

Words got me the wound
& will get me well

If you believe it.

All join now in lament
for the death of my cock
a tongue of knowledge
in the feathered night

boys get crazy in the head
& suffer
I sacrifice my cock
on the altar
of silence

❖

A WAKE

A wake
Shake dreams from your hair
     My pretty child, my sweet one
Choose the day, & the sign
     of your day,
       1st thing you see.

A burnt tree, like a giant
     primeval bird, a leaf,
dry & bitter, crackling tales
     in its warm waves.
Sidewalk gods will do for you.
     The forest of the neighborhood,
The empty lost museum, &
The mesa, & the Mt.'s pregnant
Monument above the newstand
     where the children hide
       When school ends

❖

CURSES & INVOCATIONS

Weird bait-headed mongrels
I keep expecting one of you
                              to rise
large buxom obese queens
garden hogs & cunt
                              Veterans
quaint cabbage saints
Shit horders & individualists
drag-strip officials
Tight-lipped losers
& lustful fuck salesmen
My militant dandies
all strange order of monsters
hot on the trail of the
                              wood vine
We welcome you to our
                              Procession

❖

THE CROSSROADS

Meeting you at your parent's gate
We will tell you what to do
What you have to do
to survive

Leave the rotten towns
of your father
Leave the poisoned wells
& bloodstained streets
Enter now the sweet forest

❖

I WALKED THRU...

I walked thru the panther's living room
And our summer together ended
      Too soon
Stronger than farther
Strangled by night
Rest in my sun burst
Relax in her secret wilderness
This is the sea of doubt
which threads harps
      unwithered
      & unstrung
Its the brother, not the past
who turns sunlight into glass
It's the valley
It's me

Testimony from
a strange witness

❖

THE FLOWERING

The flowering
    of god-like people
in the muted air
    would seem
        strange
to an intruder
of certain size

but this is all we have left
    to guide us
Now that He is gone

❖

THE WILD WHORE LAUGHS

The Wild whore laughs
    like an ancient spinster
Crone, we see you, come again
    in the mind
I lie like fever
    Dancing your nubile hush
willing to be possessed
    untold stories
        dare injuns rise
Trampled, like red-skins
    sacred fore-skin
Cancer began w/the knife's
    cruel blow & the damaged
rod has risen again
    in the East
        like a star
            on fire

❖

THE HITCHHIKER

(An American Pastoral)

THE SCREEN IS BLACK. We hear a young man's voice in casual conversation with friends.

> No, this guy told me you can go
> down across the border and buy a
> girl and bring her back and that's
> what I'm goin' to do, I'm gonna go
> down there and buy one of them and
> bring her back and marry her. I am.

An older woman's voice

> Billy, are you completely crazy?

We hear the good-natured laughter of the woman, a man and another friend as Billy's insistent voice rises through saying:

> BILLY
> No, it's true. Really. This guy told
> me. It's true. I'm really gonna do it.

The film changes to COLOR. A couple sit at a small table in a simulated border town nightclub. It is a CLOSE shot, reminding us possibly of Picasso's "Absinthe Drinkers." The atmosphere is suggested by peripheral sounds such as boisterous young voices, curses in a foreign language, the tinkling of glasses and music from a small rock band. Perhaps a dancer is visible in the background. Perhaps topless. An anonymous waitress could enter the frame and leave, serving drinks.

The HERO is drunk and he's trying to persuade an attractive Mexican girl, a waitress in the bar, a whore, to cross the border and marry him. The girl tolerates him. She is working, hustling drinks, and has to listen but also she likes him. In some way, he interests her.

> BILLY
>
> I bet the only reason you won't come with me is because I ain't got any money. Well, listen. I'm tellin' you. I'm gonna go back up there and get me some money, lots of it, maybe even ten thousand. And then I'm comin' back for you. I'm comin' back.

He weaves offscreen, determined, drunk, camera holds on girl, smiling wistfully and ironically after him. Then she grabs another young American and pulls him down beside her.

> THE GIRL
>
> Hey, man, you want to buy me a drink?

TITLE

> THE HITCHHIKER
> (An American Pastoral)

Film changes to BLACK and WHITE. It is dawn on the American desert; it's cold, and he stands hunched in his jacket, by the side of the highway. The sun is rising. We hold on him as a few cars go by at long intervals. We hear the car coming, watch his eyes watching, he sticks his thumb out. CUT TO profile shot, as a car swishes by. The third car stops and he runs, not too energetically and gets inside.

INTERIOR car. Middle-aged man in a business suit. He asks the hitchhiker where he is going.

> BILLY
> (mumbling)
> L.A.

He is obviously reluctant to do any talking.

> THE DRIVER
> I can take you as far as Amarillo and then you'll have to go on from there.

> BILLY
> (No reply. No recognition.)

> DRIVER
> What are you going to do when you get to L.A.? Have you got a job lined up?

BILLY
(No answer. He is beginning to nod.)

The man drives on. We see glimpses of the American land-
scape out the window of the car. The man glances sideways
occasionally at Billy who is sleeping

CLOSE UP of the man's right hand moving snake-like to-
wards the hiker's left leg. He hesitates and then touches it
above the knee. Immediately, a .38 revolver appears from
Billy's jacket and points at the driver.

BILLY
Pull over.

Profile of car, left side, extremely long shot. We hear a shot.
The hitchhiker comes around the rear of the car, opens the
door, and pulls the driver toward camera, his corpse that is,
to the gully, and, after stripping his wallet of all the cash,
gets into the car and drives away.

The kid is standing beside the car with his thumb out. The
hood is raised. The engine has failed. A State Patrolman (we
learn this from his uniform, western hat, and badge) stops in
his own unmarked car. Billy gets in the car. The sheriff is
friendly. He talks a lot. He tells Billy that he's just getting
back home after delivering two lunatics from his local jail to
the state asylum.

SHERIFF
I had to put them both in straight-
jackets and throw them in the back
of the wagon. I had to. They were
totally uninhibited. I mean, if I let
'em loose, they just start jerking off
and playing with each other, so I had
to keep them tied up.

The killer is trying to stay awake. He's strung out on ben-
nies, and also just plain exhausted, and he's fighting to fol-
low the man's conversation. The sheriff rambles on. Billy is
in that weird state between sleep and waking where it is hard
to distinguish between what's being said in reality and what
he hears in his dream. The sheriff asks a question. He an-
swers and then jerks up suddenly to realize that he's been
inventing his own dialogue inside his head. Finally, he can
take it no longer. He pulls the gun out and orders the sheriff
to pull over to the side of the road. Then he forces him to
unlock the trunk, orders him inside and slams the lid.

INTERIOR of car. The hitchhiker is driving on.

As the car slows down for an upgrade, the trunk flies open
and the sheriff tumbles out into the dust. Billy sees it in the
rearview mirror. He slams on the brakes, jumps out of the
car and runs back to the spot. From off in the desert, we see
the sheriff racing insanely toward the camera. He suddenly

leaps and throws himself flat on the ground behind a sand dune, next to the camera. From this point of view, the sheriff crouched and breathing in heavy gasps, we watch the kid stand on the side of the road, stare out into the desert and finally get back into the car and drive away.

Billy is hitchhiking again. Obviously, he has ditched the sheriff's car somewhere along the way. A car pulls over. There is a young man driving and in the back seat are his wife and two small children, a boy and a girl. The driver is friendly, tells him he used to hitchhike a lot himself and volunteers the information that he has just returned home from two years in Viet Nam, where he was a pilot. Billy pulls out the gun and lets them know immediately that he wants them to take him anywhere he wants to go. Otherwise, he'll kill them.

It is NIGHT. They pull into a gas station. Billy is hungry, so are the kids. So he goes with the ex-aviator into a small country store that's part of the station. He warns the family to keep quiet or he'll kill everyone.

INSIDE the country store. A seedy old man behind the counter. They ask him for a bunch of ham sandwiches. In close-up, we watch him slice the meat, the knife hesitating minutely, deciding on the thickness of each slice. The two men stand there watching him. Suddenly, the husband wheels around and gets a grip on the hitchhiker from behind. They whirl madly around the store, the father screaming for the proprietor to call the police.

THE MAN
Stop him! He's got a gun!! He's
gonna kill us!!! Help me!!!!

Billy somehow manages to get his gun out and forces the man to the car. The store owner stares after him, mouth agape, then picks up the receiver to call the police.

MORNING. A young boy finds the car, pulled off on a side road, splattered with blood. He opens the door and sees the little girl's baby doll, the naked, flesh-colored rubber kind, and in close-up, we see blood on it.

The EXTERIOR of a run-down shack in the country. We hear the sounds from inside. INTERIOR of shack. Television and radio and newspaper reporters, including an attractive woman with a notebook, are interviewing the killer's father. He's a very old man, an alcoholic, who is slightly pleased to be thrust suddenly into the spotlight, but who treats the situation with a grave sense of public image and self-irony.

THE FATHER
He was always a pretty strange boy,
specially after his mother passed
away. Then he got real quiet. He
didn't have many friends. Just his
brothers and sisters.

GIRL REPORTER
Mr. Cooke, is there anything you'd
like to tell your son?

FATHER
Yes, there is. Billy, if you can hear
me, son, please turn yourself in.
Cause what you're doin', it just ain't
right. You're not doin' right, son.
And you know it.

During this appeal, the camera has moved slowly into a
CLOSE-UP of the old man's face.

INTERIOR. Car. Night. Rain. A car radio. The light glows
yellow in the dark car. The radio is playing a country gospel
hour. A revival meeting. The preacher and his flock. As Billy
listens, we flash back into his past, over the rain and wind-
shield wipers. We see an old man and a young boy in the
woods. The man is Billy's father and the boy is Billy himself
at about age seven or eight. The father teaches his son how
to shoot a gun. He tells him to aim at a rabbit.

THE FATHER
Don't be afraid, son. Don't be afraid.
Just squeeze one off.

We see a rabbit pinioned in a rifle's telescopic sight.

A small town high school, 3:30, bell rings, school is out. The kids gush from the building and flow like a human stream to the favorite drive-in restaurant.

INTERIOR of car. Billy is eating a cheeseburger and Coke. Through his windows he watches the movements of one of the carhops. She is wearing slacks and with him we watch her ass and thighs. When she comes to collect, he asks her to come for a ride with him. We hear him say this but the ensuing dialogue is shown in pantomime. The actual voices are drowned out by the sounds of radios, kids talking.

They are driving up a mountain road. The Rolling Stones' "I Can't Get No Satisfaction" comes on the radio. Billy sings along with the record with wild abandon and squirms in his seat like a toad.

The car is parked on a rocky view overlooking the ocean. He gets out of the car and dances around it, acting crazy, and howling like an Indian. He ducks up and down, appearing and reappearing in different windows. She laughs at his clowning.

The couple are in the back seat, vaguely we see their movements, hear them whispering, laughing, talking. CUT TO outside of car. They get out of the back of the car, hair and clothes disarranged and move side by side into a rough terrain behind some rocks. Camera holds on the rocks. A primeval rock formation. At a rhythm that is peculiarly excruciating, we hear three gunshots.

A rest room in an LA service station. EXTERIOR. Billy enters rest room.

INTERIOR rest room. Billy shaves with soap in rest room mirror, runs his wet hands through his hair.

EXTERIOR, downtown LA. Camera follows him from a car, as he wanders through the downtown crowds of Broadway and Main Street. Many times he is lost to our view. We see him in an arcade, where he plays a pinball machine.

CLOSE-UP of pinball game in progress.

Billy in photo booth. Flash of the lights.

CLOSE-UP of four automatic photos: flash flash flash flash. Four faces of Billy.

Billy in downtown hamburger stand. He is eating, seen from behind, Gun enters frame left. He turns and sees it, stares back blankly.

CUT TO EXTERIOR, street. In hand-held confused close-up sequence, we see him dragged and shoved into the back seat of a car (police car). He is kicked and beaten. During the struggle, we hear many men's voices, gloating righteous exclamations.

MEN
So you're the little bastard that
killed all those people! (Kick) You
had a good time, didn't you? (Kick)
You really killed 'em, didn't you?

Hands cuffed behind his back, he looks up with a confused expression and says:

BILLY
But I'm a good boy.

The men laugh.

Film switches to COLOR. A montage of extant photographs representing death. The body of Che Guevara, a northern Renaissance Dutch crucifixion, bullfight, slaughterhouse, mandalas and into abstraction. A nature film of a mongoose killing a cobra, a black dog runs free on the beach. FADE INTO BLACKNESS.

EXTERIOR night. On the steps of City Hall of Justice we see the hitchhiker descend dreamlike in slow motion, move languorously across a deserted city square toward the camera until he covers the lens and seems to pass through it.

Seen now from behind, as he moves away from lens, he enters a desert outskirt region where he finds an automobile graveyard. He is wandering in Eternity. In the junkyard, three people squat around a small fire. They're cooking potatoes in the coals, an older man named DOC pokes the fire with a stick. There is an older woman, funky, glamorous, and the third person is a young boy, a mute, of indeterminate age. He is slightly made up with white makeup. They are hoboes in Eternity and are not surprised to see him. He nears the fire.

DOC
Well, how ya doin', kid? I see you
did it again. Ya hungry? There's
some food here if ya want it.

Billy doesn't speak. He stares at the moon. The woman has
kept her head down, her hair covering her face.

DOC
Billy's back. Blue Lady, didja hear
me? I said Billy's back.

She looks up for the first time.

BLUE LADY
Hi, Billy.

BILLY
Hello, Blue Lady.

He looks at the boy.

Hiya, Clown Boy.

CLOWN BOY claps his hands and nods, his face contorted
grotesquely in greeting. They sit for a while like this, and
stare at the fire. They eat the potatoes. Then Doc rises and
says:

DOC
The sun's gonna be up in a while. I
guess we'd better move on.

Slowly, one by one, the other two rise. Doc puts out the fire
with dirt and says:

DOC
Ya comin' with us, Billy?

BILLY
(thinking hard)
I don't know, Doc, I just don't know.

Doc smiles.

DOC
Well, we'll see ya later, kid. The rest
of the gang will be real glad to see
ya. They sure will. Well . . .

Doc, Clown Boy and the Blue Lady start moving toward
the rising sun into the mountain desert. Every now and then
they turn and wave, Clown Boy leaping up and down madly
and waving good-bye.

As they slowly disappear, camera changes focus to Billy, the
hitchhiker, the kid, the killer, hunkered over the dead smol-
dering fire.

THE END

❖

Poems from
DRY WATER

IN THIS DIM CAVE

In this dim cave
we can go no further.
Here money is key
to smooth age. Horses,
givers of guilt. Great
bags of gold.

I want obedience!

We examine this ancient
& insane theatre, obscene
like luxuriant churches
altars.

I confess
to scarves
cool floors
stroked curtain

The actors are twice-blessed
before us. This is
too serious & severe.

Great mystery!
Timeless passion
patterned in stillness.

❖

SEX FOR YOU

Sex for you
was thread
which binds
us even now
on this pale
planet.

To the poet
& cover-girl,
photo in color,
to armies
that join,
out on a desert,
& to Samson
& all his
generals
bound quiet
now w/exotic
arch-angels
of dusk, in
Sumarian
& N. African
slumbers.

The bazaar is crowded
as dancers thrive.
Snake-wreaths & pleasures.
I take you to a low cave
called "Calipah".

STAND THERE LISTENING

Stand there listening
you will hear them
tiny shapes just beyond
          the moon
Star-flys, jarts,
dismal fronds
stirring ape-jaws striving
to make the morning
mail call

Cry owl.
Hark to the wood-vine.
Suckle-snake crawls, gnawing
restive

I know you.
The one who left to go
warning. Wishless now
& sullen. Transfer
deferred.

Steal me a peach
from the orange tree
grove-keeper

She fell.

STAND THERE LISTENING

What are you doing
w/your hand on her
breast?

She fell, mam.

Give her to me.

Yes, mam.

Go tell the master
what you've done.

They killed him.

Later.

Going up the stairs
handcuffed
to his cell.

A shot-gun blast
Behind the back.

❖

UNTRAMPLED FOOTSTEPS

I

Untrampled footsteps
Borderline dreams
Occasion for sinners
alive if it seems
given to wander
alone at the shore
wanton to whisper
I am no more
Am as my heart beats
live as I can
wanton to whisper
faraway sands

II

Now come into my pretty isle
My weary westward wanderer
Faraway is as it seems
& so alone shall shelter
Come along unto my sails
as weary islands go
prosper merry as I went
I shall no more the sailor
Shall I ho the sailor

UNTRAMPLED FOOTSTEPS

III

Where were you when I needed you?
Where indeed but in some sheltered
Sturdy heaven; wasted, broken
sadly broke & one thin thing to get us thru

UNTRAMPLED FOOTSTEPS

IV

Urchin crawl broke
        spenders bleeders all
brew North
        stained lot
he was lost
        out on an aircraft
high above
        long awkward brewer's
                shelters breed

this ugly crew
        our poisoned jet
god get us love & get
        us speed
To get us home again
        love
Crippled by people
        cut by nothing
Public housing
        the incredible damage
                can be cured

UNTRAMPLED FOOTSTEPS

V

She's my girl friend:
I wouldn't tell her
        Name but I think
you already know her
        Name
            is
Square fire insect
marble saffron intro
demi-rag in flames

it's the same game
whether you call it
by her real name

UNTRAMPLED FOOTSTEPS

VI

She lives in the city
       under the sea
Prisoner of pirates
       prisoner of dreams
I want to be w/her
       want her to see
The things I've created
       sea-shells that bleed
Sensitive seeds
       of impossible warships

Dragon-fly hovers
       & wavers & teases
The weeds & his wings
       are in terrible fury

❖

LYRIC VERSE

MOONLIGHT DRIVE

Let's swim to the moon
Let's climb thru the tide
Penetrate the evenin'
That the city sleeps to hide
Let's swim out tonight, love
It's our turn to try
Parked beside the ocean
On our moonlight drive.

Let's swim to the moon
Let's climb thru the tide
Surrender to the waiting worlds
That lap against our side.
Nothin' left open
And no time to decide,
We've stepped into a river
On our moonlight drive.

Let's swim to the moon
Let's climb thru the tide
You reach your hand to hold me
But I can't be your guide.
Easy, I love you
As I watch you glide,
Falling through wet forests
On our moonlight drive.
Midnight moonlight drive.

MOONLIGHT DRIVE

Come on, baby, gonna take a little ride,
Down, down by the ocean side.
Gonna get real close,
Get real tight,
Baby gonna drown tonight.
Goin' down, down, down.

❖

Words and Music by The Doors
Copyright © 1967, Doors Music Co.

TO BE ALONE

To be alone
& watch the dawn
  It could create
  a silly song
About a girl
  I used to know

She was the star
  of the lost side show

She wasn't me
She wasn't you
Believe you me
Knew what to do

& say to a man on
the end of his tether
"Hey, fine handsome
Man, there'll be a change
in the weather"

So what am I
Supposed to do
Just sit alone
& chew my shoe
I need a love
No more than she
& yet no less
& no regrets

TO BE ALONE

If you can fill me in
on my Telephone
I'd be a sadder,
wiser son of a gun

I'll just this
about all that
I was the mouse
who caught the cat

I don't intend
To give you no points
of view

I just mean to tell
You—I'm alone

❖

SOUL KITCHEN

Well, the clock says it's time to close—now,
I guess I'd better go—now,
I'd really like to stay here all night.
The cars crawl past all stuffed with eyes,
Street lights share their hollow glow,
Your brain seems bruised with numb surprise,
Still one place to go,
Still one place to go.

CHORUS
Let me sleep all night in your soul kitchen
Warm my mind near your gentle stove
Turn me out & I'll wander baby
Stumblin' in the neon groves.

Well, your fingers weave quick minarets
Speak in secret alphabets
I light another cigarette
Learn to forget, learn to forget,
Learn to forget, learn to forget.

CHORUS

Well the clock says it's time to close now,
I know I have to go now,
I really want to stay here
All night, all night, all night

SOUL KITCHEN

Let me sleep all night in your soul kitchen
Warm my mind near your gentle stove
Turn me out & I'll wander baby
Stumblin' in the neon groves.

❖

Words and Music by The Doors
Copyright © 1967, Doors Music Co.

WOMAN IN THE WINDOW

I am the woman
In the window
See the children
Playing

Soldier, Sailor
Young man
on your way
To the summer
Swimming pool

Can you see me
Standing
in my window
Can you hear me
laughing

       (woman's voice)
    (Come upstairs, sir
       To your room
         I will play for you)

O dreamland
Golden scene land
Try to sleep lamb
Take us to dreamland

I am unhappy
Far from my woman
Take me to dreamland
Land of the Banyon

WOMAN IN THE WINDOW

Land of plentiful
Pleasures of pines
& potatoes on tables
Laden w/good things

Eat at my table
She cried to the vineyards
Calling the workers
Home from the meadows

Man you are evil
get out of my garden
ours is a good place
Home of the rain deer

Sell me your pony
Your fast golden pony
I need his strength
& his terrible footsteps

Riding the prairie
Just me & my angel
Just try & stop us
We're going to love

Open your window
Woman of Palestine
Throw down your raiment
& cover us over.

❖

WHEN THE MUSIC'S OVER

When the music's over,
When the music's over,
When the music's over
Turn out the lights,
Turn out the lights,
Turn out the lights.

For the music is your special friend
Dance on fire as it intends
Music is your only friend
Until the end
Until the end
Until the end

Cancel my subscription
    to the Resurrection.
Send my credentials
    to the house of detention,
I got some friends inside.

The face in the mirror won't stop,
The girl in the window won't drop.
A feast of friends
"Alive," she cried,
Waitin' for me
Outside.

WHEN THE MUSIC'S OVER

Before I sink into the big sleep,
I want to hear, I want to hear
   the scream of the butterfly.

Come back, baby,
Back into my arms.

We're gettin' tired of hangin' around,
Waitin' around, with our heads to the ground.
I hear a very gentle sound,
Very near, yet very far,
Very soft, yeah, very clear,
Come today, come today.

What have they done to the earth?
What have they done to our fair sister?
Ravaged and plundered
   and ripped her and bit her,
Stuck her with knives
   in the side of the dawn,
And tied her with fences,
   and dragged her down.

I hear a very gentle sound,
With your ear down to the ground.
We want the world and we want it . . .
We want the world and we want it,
now, now, NOW!

WHEN THE MUSIC'S OVER

Persian night, babe,
See the light, babe,
Save us,
Jesus,
Save us.

So when the music's over,
When the music's over,
When the music's over
Turn out the lights,
Turn out the lights,
Turn out the lights.

Well, the music is your special friend
Dance on fire as it intends
Music is your only friend
Until the end
Until the end
Until
The end.

❖

Words and Music by The Doors
Copyright © 1967, Doors Music Co.

There's blood in the streets
& its' up to my ankles
Blood in the streets
& its up to my knee
Blood in the streets
of the town of chicago
Blood on the rise
& its following me —
Blood in the streets
runs a river of sadness
Blood in the streets
& its up to my thigh
The river runs red
down the legs of the city
The women are crying
red rivers of weeping

THERE'S BLOOD IN THE STREETS

There's blood in the streets
    & it's up to my ankles
Blood in the streets
    & its up to my knee
Blood in the streets
    of the town of Chicago
Blood on the rise
    & its following me

Blood in the streets
    runs a river of sadness
Blood in the streets
    & its up to my thigh
The river runs red
    down the legs of the city
The women are crying
    red rivers of weeping

Blood in the streets
    in the town of New Haven
Blood stains the roofs
    and the palm trees of Venice

Blood in my love
    in the terrible summer
The Bloody red sun
    of phantastic L.A.

THERE'S BLOOD IN THE STREETS

Blood! screams her brain
    as they chop off her fingers
Blood will be born
    in the birth of a Nation
Blood is the rose of mysterious
                union.

❖

Words and Music by The Doors
Copyright © 1970, Doors Music Co.

THE END

This is the end, beautiful friend.
This is the end, my only friend,
the end,
   of our elaborate plans,
the end,
   of everything that stands,
the end,
   no safety or surprise,
the end.
I'll never look into your eye again.

Can you picture what will be,
so limitless and free
desperately in need
of some stranger's hand,
in a desperate land.

Lost in a Roman wilderness of pain,
and all the children are insane,
all the children are insane
waiting for the summer rain.

There's danger on the edge of town,
Ride the King's highway.
Weird scenes inside the gold mine;
Ride the highway west, baby.

THE END

Ride the snake.
Ride the snake,
To the lake, the ancient lake.
The snake is long, seven miles.
Ride the snake,
He's old, and his skin is cold.

The west is the best,
The west is the best,
Get here and we'll do the rest.
The blue bus is calling us,
The blue bus is calling us,
Driver where you taking us?

The killer awoke before dawn,
He put his boots on.
He took a face from the ancient gallery,
And he walked on down the hall.

He went into the room
where his sister lived and,
then he
paid a visit to his brother,
and then he,
he walked on down the hall.

And he came to a door,
And he looked inside,
"Father?"
"Yes, son?"
"I want to kill you.
Mother, I want to . . ."

THE END

Come on, baby, take a chance with us,
Come on, baby, take a chance with us,
Come on, baby, take a chance with us
And meet me at the back of the blue bus.

This is the end, beautiful friend,
This is the end, my only friend,
the end,
 it hurts to set you free,
 but you'll never follow me.
The end
 of laughter and soft lies,
The end
 of nights we tried to die.
This is the end.

❖

Words and Music by The Doors
Copyright © 1967, Doors Music Co.

L.A. WOMAN

Well, I just got into town about
            an hour ago
Took a look around, see which
            way the wind blow
Where the little girls in their
            Hollywood bungalows

Are you a lucky little lady in
            The City of Light?
Or just another lost angel
            City of Night
            City of Night
            City of Night
            City of Night

L.A. Woman
L.A. Woman
L.A. Woman Sunday afternoon
L.A. Woman Sunday afternoon
L.A. Woman Sunday afternoon
Drive thru your suburbs
Into your blues
Into your blues
Into your blue–blue Blues
Into your blues

L.A. WOMAN

I see your hair is burning
Hills are fill'd w/fire
If they say I never lov'd you
You know they are a liar
Drivin' down your freeways
Midnite alleys roam
Cops in cars, the topless bars
Never saw a woman—
So alone
So alone
So alone
So alone

Motel money murder madness
Let's change the mood from glad
                    to sadness

Mr. Mojo Risin' (4x)
Got to keep on risin'
Mr. Mojo Risin' (5x)
Got to keep on risin'
Risin' risin' (5x)

Well, I just got into town about
            an hour ago
Took a look around, see which
            way the wind blow
Where the little girls in their
            Hollywood bungalows

JIM MORRISON

L. A. WOMAN

Are you a lucky little lady in
                The City of Light?
Or just another lost angel
                City of Night
                City of Night
                City of Night
                City of Night

L.A. Woman
L.A. Woman
L.A. Woman
You're my woman
Little L.A. Woman
Little L.A. Woman

❖

Music by The Doors
Copyright © 1971, Doors Music Co.

❖

NOTEBOOK POEMS

*There are images I need to
complete my own reality*

TALES OF THE AMERICAN NIGHT

Discovery
Angels & Sailors   (rich girls)
Backyard fences, tents
dreams watching each other
narrowly
Soft luxuriant cars
Girls in garages
stripped, out to get
liquor & clothes
Half-gallons of wine
& six-packs of beer
Tender corral.   Jumped.
Humped.   Born to suffer.
Made to undress in
        the wilderness

❖

— Hey man you want girls
pills grass come-on
& show you good time
This place has everything
come-on, & show you

Burlesque Beat

Can we resolve the past — lurking jaws
joints of Time — the base — to come
of age in a dry place — holes & cave

The music was new black polished
chrome & came over the summer
like liquid night — The D.J.'s
Took pills to stay awake & play
for 7 days.

The General's son had a sister.
They went down to see him.
They went to the studio & someone
knew ~~theee~~ him. Some one knew
The T.V. showman.

CAN WE RESOLVE THE PAST

—Hey man you want girls
  Pills   grass   come-on
  I show you good time
  This place has everything
  Come-on, I show you

   Burlesque Beat

Can we resolve the past – lurking jaws
joints of Time – the base – to come
of age in a dry place – holes & caves

The music was new black polished
chrome & came over the summer
like liquid night – the D.J.'s
Took pills to stay awake & play
for 7 days.

The General's son had a sister.
They went down to see him.
They went to the studio & someone
knew him.   Someone knew
the T.V. Showman.

CAN WE RESOLVE THE PAST

He came to our home room party &
played records & when he left,
in the hot noon sun, & walked
to his car, we saw the Chooks
had written F–U–C–K on his
windshield. He wiped it off
w/a white rag &, smiling cooly,
drove away.

"He's rich. Got a big car."

My friend drove an hour each day
    from the Mts. The bus gives
you a hard-on w/books in your
lap. We shot the bird at the
    black M.P.

My gang will get you.   Scenes
of rape in the arroyo.   Seductions
in cars, abandoned buildings.
Fights at the food stand.
The dust. The Shoes
Opened shirts & raised collars.
Bright sculptured hair.
Spades dance best, from the hip.

Someone shot the bird on the
afternoon dance show. They gave
out free records to the best
couple.

❖

ALWAYS A PLAYGROUND INSTRUCTOR

Always a playground instructor,
never a killer. Always a bridesmaid
on the verge of fame, or over,
he maneuvered 2 girls into his
hotel room.   One, a friend,
and a newer stranger, vaguely
Mexican or Puerto Rican.

Poor boy's thighs & buttocks, scarred
by a father's belt. She's trying
to rise. Story of her boyfriend
& teen-age stone death games.
Handsome cat, dead in a car.

Come here
I love you.
Peace on earth
Will you die for me
eat me
this way
the end

ALWAYS A PLAYGROUND INSTRUCTOR

—I'm surprised you could get it up.
He whips her lightly, sardonically
w/belt.
—Haven't I been thru enough? she asks.

The dark girl begins to bleed.
It's Catholic heaven. I have an
ancient Indian crucifix around
my neck. My chest is hard
& brown. Lying on stained &
wretched sheets w/a bleeding Virgin.
We could plan a murder, or
    Start a religion.

❖

I WANT TO TELL YOU

I want to tell you
about
Texas Radio & the Big Beat

it comes out of the Virgin Swamps
cool & slow
w/plenty of precision
& a back beat narrow
& hard to master
some call it heavenly
in its brilliance
others mean & rueful
of the Western dream

I love the friends I have
    gathered together
On this thin raft
we have constructed pyramids
    in honor of our escaping
This is the land where
    The pharaoh died—
Children
The river contains specimens
The voices of singing women
call us on the far shore

& they are saying
"Forget the Night
live w/us in Forests
of azure"   (meager food for
                            souls forgot)

JIM MORRISON

I WANT TO TELL YOU

I tell you this;
    no eternal reward will
forgive us now for
    wasting the dawn

One morning you awoke
& the strange sun
& opening your door . . .

❖

Music by The Doors
Copyright © 1971, Doors Music Co.

NOW LISTEN TO THIS

"Now listen to this:
I'll tell you about
Texas Radio & the Big Beat
Soft driven slow & mad
like some new language

Reaching your head
w/the cold & sudden fury
of a divine messenger
Let me tell you about
            heartache & the loss
                        of God
Wandering, wandering
in hopeless night

The negroes in the forest
brightly feathered
let me show you the maiden
w/wrought-iron soul
Out here on the perimeter
there are no stars
Out here we is stoned
            immaculate"

❖

Music by The Doors
Copyright © 1971, Doors Music Co.

TIME WORKS LIKE ACID

Time works like acid
Stained eyes
You see time fly

The face changes as the heart beats
& breathes

We are not constant
We are an arrow in flight
The sum of the angles of change

Her face changed in the car
eyes & skin & hair remain
the same. But a hundred similar
girls succeed each other

❖

THE SIDEWALKERS MOVED...

        The sidewalkers moved faster
We joined the current. Suddenly
the cops, plastic shields & visors,
wielding long thin truncheons
like wands, in formation,
clearing the street the other way.
To get near or stay away.
Cafes were taking in tables
putting chairs on upside
down, pulling the steel playpen
safety bars. Whistles as
the vans arrive. Moustached
soldiers. We leave the scene.
Eyes of youth, wary, gleaming.
The church. A pastoral scene
of guitars, drums, flutes,
harps, & lovers. Past
Shakespeare & Co., the restaurants
w/elegant patrons, cross

THE SIDEWALKERS MOVED...

street, the small Jazz
district (Story Ville) a
miniature New Orleans.
Negroes in African shirts.
A street brass band.
"Fare well to my web footed friends"
Crowd smiles, jogs, & sings.
Move past. San Michel Blvd.
The Statue. The Seine. Bonfires
of cardboard buzz evilly,
down the blvd. Fire-tenders.
Smell of smoke. Approach closer
nearer. Suddenly screams
long warhoops & the crowd runs
back. And as we flee,
they attack from behind,
Pressed against cafe tables.
Subway & news Kiosk – A
girl beaten, her cries. Can't
hear blows.   Rain.   (Man w/bottle)
Join me at the demonstration

We join groups under trees
& rain. Tall public buildings.

Join us at the demonstration

❖

Dreams are at once fruit & outcry
against an atrophy of the senses.

Dreaming is no solution

WE AWOKE, TALKING...

We awoke, talking. Telling dreams.
an explosion during the night

A new siren. Not cop, Fire,
New York ambulance or european
movie riot news but the strange
siren predicting war. She ran
to the window. The yellow thing
had risen.

FEAR IS A PORCH...

Fear is a porch where winds
    slide thru in the North
A face at the Window that
    becomes a leaf
An eagle sensing its disaster
But soaring gracefully above
A rabbit shining in the night

❖

STILL WET FROM...

Still wet from a strange dream
dawn burst
scarring the chamber's
roof where all things lie

I sat w/her & sipped cold sherry

Airport.

(Caesura = ante-room to hell)

❖

START AGAIN

Start again: Should the events of those
days . . .   Dream of incest & expulsion
from the tribe.   Big Sister.   It's called
the clap.   Get on over here, mother-of-pearl.
I was a virgin.   It lasted 10 seconds.
Well don't then.   "I can't relax."   Roll the
leather pants up tightly for the morrow
                                        hour.
They deserted me, deserted the cause, message
or word for another god.   "We're kicking
you out of our universe!"   He ask'd for you.
I'll bet he did.

❖

Start again. Should the events of those days...! Dream of incest & expulsion from the tribe. Big sister. It's called the clap. Get on over here, mother-of-pearl. I was a virgin. It lasted 15 seconds. Well don't them. 'I can't relax.' Roll the leather pants up tightly for the morrow. They deserted me...how? another on word for the goods. 'We're licking you out of our own universe!' He asked for you; I'll bet he did.

MYSTERY OF THE DREAM

Mystery of the dream
a woman or girl is trying
to appear

The Killer—Mexican, naked
except for shoes.

People, a family not connected
move at hypnotic cross lines
out of still frame

2 men, detectives, following
searching, sifting thru
back & side lit rooms, holding
muted counsel. Hats, suits.
Brothers.

People in a wood, a park.
The Killer lurks in his
own world.

dreams of children & families
return to the sub-world
to assimilate & guide events

New Orleans, sleep, (death's
friend, death's sister)
cattle, horses
faces get rubbery, clown-painted,
stupid sly & wise & knowing

MYSTERY OF THE DREAM

The mystery of flight
To be inside the brain of a bird
goal—the end of a goddess
   to slide gracefully &
knowledgeably into graveland
The Big dream
      vs
Violent assassination of
   Spirit & neck & skull
wounded he arrived

❖

THE DARK AMERICAN SUNSET

The dark American Sunset
The night like a vast
conspiracy to dream, hold
court in the swaying sand

Tijuana—the anus of Night
a cartoon of civilization
Whores are bores in the
American Night

What will we see in the
bowels of the night, in
The frosted cave where dreams
are made, right before your
eyes. Prophecy w/out money.

This song must have the sad
common strangeness of currency
coin of the realm. Bitter
embers. Scent of pine smoke
Fire-Night, special breeding
exercises. An excuse for
crime. High School of the
Night. Silence of a school
at night.

❖

L'AMERICA

Acid dreams & Spanish Queens
      L'america (another?, lone?, voice)
Asthma child, the fumidor
      Lamerica
Duchess, rabbit, the woods by the road
      Lamerica
Pearl Harbor—Shot off the road
      Lamerica
Conceived in a beach Town
      Lamerica
Relevance of beach or Lakes
      Lamerica
Sinks, snakes, caves w/water
      Florida
Homo/-sex/-uality
      Lamerica
Religion & the Family
      Lamerica
Plane crash in the Eastern Woods
      Virginia
Bailing-out over rice-fields
      Lamerica
Guerrilla band inside the town
      Lamerica
Bitter tree of consciousness
      Lamerica
A fast car in the night—the road
      Lamerica
Progress of The Good Disease
      Lamerica

❖

AMERICA AS BULLRING ARENA

Those indians, dreams, &
the cosmic spinal bebop in blue.
The cosmic horrors. The cosmic
heebeejeebies. A combo of brain
tissue, blood, shit, sweat
sperm & steel, mixed w/grease
& liquid fire, ovaric calendars
Magnified on inner
Television lust-face, mirrors
into Nothing, great silence
opens layers of prehistoric
chinese monsters. The mouths,
the mouths, the cellular MAW.
A young Witch from
N.Y. is laying novice hexes
on my brain-pan, projecting
images of embryo development
on my psychology.

Her terrified wildness
disturbs my generals.
Baby, now I dig your
nightmare visions, & your
sadness & your bitchery

But, yet, thank you for
These spells. It gets my
pen moving.

AMERICA AS BULLRING ARENA

The screaming maggot
group-grope called life.

It's time for the desert wild.

Lust capital.

Time for an island, get
drunk, write & sail.

"I saw the Hell of women
back there."

Women are obsolete

"Little Wine—dig that girl"

We placate women w/
food & song
w/sex, marriage, babies

You dig kids, Jim

Yeah, some of them are nice

I like your wife

Democracy of souls

❖

THE GUIDED TOUR

The guided tour
"I am a guide to the labyrinth"

city is inside of body made manifest
meat organs & electrical
power plants

The place where, walking down
death-row ("You look like you're"),
maps – AMERICUS – a river-vein
we ride along.

give form to the passing world

Freeways are a drama, a new
art form. Signs. Houses.
Faces. Loud gabble of Blacks
at a bus-stop.

❖

CAR CEMETERY

car cemetery
The abandoned cars
The color of car paint, new at night
under neon
The dead reside in cars
—the old man, filthy,
        keeper of the graveyard
Children, curious, throw stones

❖

PLEASE LIKE ME

please like me
        says the shrew
what can I do?
        I love her.

❖

WOMAN'S VOICE

Woman's Voice:
  The palace of sperm seems warm tonight

Man:
  Umm. gloom gloom doom ruin.

Woman:
  Marble porches. The grand ball room.
  Silver smiles. Trumpets. Dancing

Man
  I want only you

Woman
  This time come in me like an astronaut
  Send snakes in my orbit

Man
  We can accomplish miracles
      when we're together.

Woman
  Alone

Man
  w/the night to guide us

❖

DON'T START THAT...

Don't start that panic
Love Street parade

No one's afraid of the law

Someone escaped
To the shore

Your image of me / my image of you
        in
one-night scenes
out on the coast

Won't work anymore

Soft parade
Love Street brigade

I BRING THESE...

I bring these few rags
   back home this evening
& lay them at your feet
Miserable witness
   to a day of tragic
   sadness & disbelief
Hope you'll find me wanting
Take me to bed
Get me drunk (lay me out)

❖

THE WEDDING-DRESS

The bride-to-be lies in her bed
listening to
Festivities below
He steals her—in a dream

❖

STAR FISH GLUTTONY

Star fish gluttony
What are the word-forms
   for co(s)mic encounter
wedding flesh & mind
    in one body

❖

TENDER ISLAND NIGHT

Tender island Night
And a promise of fever
& scars that burst
          at blossom depths
& more green silver

Us wrestling in the warm temple of summer
beside the temple
cool inside
—He took my hand.
   He spoke to me—

Black horse hooves galloping sun
mad chariot race burning
mad fiery chariot race
mad girl & mad boy
My feathered son flew
          too near to the sun.

❖

A MOVING

a moving
　　　or movement
　　　　　away from
　　　　　　　a station

　　　　　　　　(weigh station)

Sound of lone car & low radio

A waving [good–bye to relations]
　　　a way from
　　　　　a waving
　　　　　　　a motion

amazement
　　　a moment
　　　　　amazing
　　　　　　　a waving

　　　(call radio breaks in)

Uh, we have a message
　　　　　brak brak

❖

HE FOLLOWS A WOMAN...

He follows a woman into the firmament
The solids, sonnets
elaborate requisitions for the god-soul

ah my bright jewelled town
a Widow's band
roping sailors & hill-folk together
congeal on this flat spire
to partakc of mineral jets
"he's sick" he should be sleeping
peaceful by air, a movie of dead nights
in a wound, suffer to give out
your red–blue lighter's flame
w/calm precision
your certainty lives in a match
or a mind
The huts are free evening cliff-dwellers
The trees, losing their variance, die sadly
w/grandeur
O soft redness & palest blue
      like a babie's window
      This is the hour you rule
   & invite Ventures, quests,
   trips to the electric valley down

❖

PROMISES

"Mana Man"

He gets them into the dark hour
By playing singing stories hypnosis
wilderness   the island
Led out of bondage   (back there)
Viciously peeling fruit

Disguised as "Players"
command Performance

See-thru village
old hot forest of cars

cruel ambience
Leopard snake dance

swift lions of doubt
crouch in the window
& wait
for her to come

❖

DO YOU HAVE

do you have
         straight jackets
for the guests
         yes we do

❖

JIM MORRISON

HORSE LATITUDES

When the still sea conspires an armor
And her sullen and aborted
Currents breed tiny monsters,
True sailing is dead.

Awkward instant
And the first animal is jettisoned,
Legs furiously pumping
Their stiff green gallop,
And heads bob up
Poise
Delicate
Pause
Consent
In mute nostril agony
Carefully refined
And sealed over

❖

Words and Music by The Doors
Copyright © 1967, Doors Music Co.

THE ORIGINAL TEMPTATION...

The original temptation was to destroy.
The Cliffs. The Road. The Walls.
Original heroism—to bluff the elements
of fire. To call creatures into the storm.
The original heroism was to fall. To ball.
The All. Natural man.

To participate in the creation.
To screw things up. To bring Things
into being.

The Crossroads where the car hides.
Lies. Resides. A meeting-place
of Worlds. Where dreams are made.
Where anything is possible. Demons
lie.

The car is steel & chrome. The wood-pile.
Top of the pile. The heap. The graveyard.
Where metal is reduced to its common
mute element. To be reborn. A tale
of rebirth in the wilderness. To become
chaos & come back.

2 spade chicks, or a king & queen,
comment from the balcony.

The types of society pass on the boards.
Microcosm in a thimble

❖

TIMES CHANGE, DAMAGED

times change, damaged
cat's blood rectify in haste
cactus furrows, wild
thrift catalog of grace

The chase bore inward
raise'd wet & westward shadows
To the strange trust
on the south bow

Augment pure shouter's drawl
& light the candle
Night is comin' on
& we're outnumbered

By the waves, each soldier
bristling w/his trowel
To search & claim us
Teach our burial

The mind works wonders
for a spell, the lantern breathes
enlightens, then farewell

TIMES CHANGE, DAMAGED

Each shipmate oars to under-
stand & eyes unoptic strains
to hear:

Wc camc from over here,
      to over there

Then told we wonder
mindless to degree
Most seldom furls
in slumber, burns
begins a century

❖

PLANES ARE GROANING MOTHERS

Planes are groaning mothers
In our feeble insect wars.

Nylon condoms stream behind her Trojan
Warriors on their dreadful writhing flight.

Bailed out, sucked
from her metal belly,
one thin wire is left to prophesy return,
jump freely.

Swallowing air in the brief canal.
The ground leaps up like dogs
to snap, the field, & rolling pain.

Swamps, rice fields, danger.
Gunned down, over ten of them
struggling w/the wet placenta

While some land back in oceans.
Skin-divers float, free-float,
in the uterus.

The sea is a Vagina which
may be penetrated at any point.

❖

AH, THE RULE...

Ah, the rule was war, as friendship
faltered. Families quarrelled, as usual,
in their chambers. The race suffered.
We traveled. We left home & beauty.
Ah, into these ships, again, we hastened.
The creation of power is slow-wasted.
Borrowed fillings. Brace for the brine.
Heaven kept, hour dated. Winds fermented
madness & kept parlour rife & rancid.

       Crews took leave of sour concubines
& habits. The sea is no place for a lady.
Lads larked & frolicked, pulvering waves
they would seek into the deep. Ark! Ark!
Cathay or Venice. Worlds beyond, &
Worlds after.

       This story has no moral.
Trust not sleep or sorrow.
The fife-man croons the lull to wake
& Brings strong soldiers to a windy beach

❖

ENSENADA

India ink, ink of India
There are no more rich colors
Black neon, blocks away,
Escapes back smooth
in the desert sea.

There's an appearance of sweat
on Italian silk skin.
Slap the rude face, & twist
into the doorway.

Then reappear, w/drums & glass
in jewels of laughter as one
called "The Gladiator,"
Hair claimed by flame of fire

(Insulting to be back.
 The dreaded, dismal day.)

Jail is a pussy coil,
dry as meat, dog-faced,
clever.

(Handsome dog & the shot gun eye.)

ENSENADA

We leap the wall, dog & I,
To hang choking on fence collar chain.
Mate follows leap to suffer
String-throat, hollow, madness cry.

(In this "hollow" we were born.)

Mexican Khaki, the green womb.
Distrust all lovely words like green & womb.

(Obey the father.
 Run.)

Escape back into the landscape,
dry as meat, dusty, narrow.

Dog licks shit
Mexican girl whore sucks my prick.

(Open windows on the town.
 Open pores on foreign air.)

The car rasps quiet.
Motor destroys itself on rotten fuel.
The pump is ill.
The hose has a steel nozzle.

❖

FLESH OF HER...

Flesh of her rolls flesh away
in waves, The waters part
dry scalps beneath the hair
nude-white & very rare

And when she exits bed, the barge
To bathe in ocean's tile & under
surgeon's glare, blinking
I bask on the red floor of a Red Sea

Crime begins in the bed, the home,
It's a low tide that talks
to rocks, & leaves
rust in its wake, & dry things crackling.

❖

I FUCKED THE DREGS...

I fucked the dregs of the ruins
          of an empire
I fucked the dust and the
          horrible queen
I fucked the chick at the
          gates of the Maya
I fucked all your women
          & treated the same
w/respect for your warriors
          returned from the
             Kingdom
fucked w/the Negroes
          in cabs of the drivers
Fucked little infants of North
          Indo-China
Branded w/Napalm & screaming
          in pain

❖

I Fucked the dregs of the ruins
            of an empire
I Fucked the dust & the
            horrible queen
I Fucked the chick at the
            gates of the Maya
I Fucked all your women
            & treated the same
w/ respect for your warriors
            returned from the
                    Kingdom
Fucked w/ the Negroes
            in cabs of the drivers
Fucked little infants of North
                    Indo-China
Branded w/ Napalm & screaming
                    in pain

PENCILLED HEAVEN

pencilled heaven
my regards
no when to stop

❖

THERE'S SOMEONE AT THE DOOR

There's someone at the door.
A rapist rushes in.
No pain. No death.

It's us, over & over again.

We're coming in.
All right, search the place.
You won't find anything.

Seeing all perspectives at once.

When everything freezes
& kind of turns back
in on itself.

❖

FEAST GREEN BEAST...

feast green beast, spurred on by
sex, seasoned in silence, w/held
from slumber, silent in the deep pale
night beast languid a cool a cunt
a forest flower awoken now breathe
utter a word of reproach for fair
swifty flyers agon of night
The dream car the outlaw star
now he sits reclines in a terrible mansion
made more monstrous by the dark stroke
of slumber

The car is a purple foil beast dead in the
night.   Neon is its sign his rich home
soft luxuriant car death gave grace
shaken to the soil   He stood in a strange
centre by the meeting pt. of worlds
This crossroads of desert flies the
corpse of sand batteries the ignition
What did happen!   He screams at camera
Here she lie bleeding, blue wounds
just to tell us in our floppy hats
it's over.   The cops are rubber animals
w/surgeons cold pride, w/out their
glamour.   The ambulance attendants
are sudden amateurs, good-natured in
this foreign chore.   The cliffs no longer
contain faces.   "I know what jail is
like" & "I know about time."

FEAST GREEN BEAST...

So we played the carnival.   Car.   Carne.
Feast of meat.   Celebration of blood.

O lucky ones who enjoy the dumb show

The reptile farm.   The snake farm.
Woman & Monkey.   The sign.   The sign.

Search for the Tree.   The place.   The sink
Big Dismal

Goes in 2 ways.   Spirit & Meat.   (sex)
You cannot join what can't be joined
You cannot travel 2 roads
        (He road off in all directions)

Hand Grenade

❖

VERY BRAVE

Very brave
   all the rage
      to tempt loneliness
        upon Front page
        gold head lines
   w/ Ali Khan & all the rest
      Onassis, Blues
   BB Albert Collins
      gin & tonic
   give him a high martin i
       get him down
          the prancing clown
will bring the empire
   swooping swirling
Tunnelling Thundering Tumbling
       hell, O, down

(That's as down as I can
   get right now, on a
   Mainstream, & I am pretty
   high, far gone)

VERY BRAVE

Thank god I have the
Sweet warm promise of
a woman there to keep
me warm

So this is where my fine warm
poetry (pottery) has got
me,
led me
back to Madness
& the men who made
me

❖

YOU THINK I DON'T KNOW...

You think I don't know that!

your poetry is so obsessed
I like my madmen cold

The abandoned Hotel
flowers dirt on its walls
The labyrinth of bowels
Moves slowly in grim waste
Children play here, wait
& sway here, tiring to her
swoon arched summer
and languid by the bow
Sits Esther, made up
like a queen, port in
a storm, striking fire-bells
in her drawers, chalking
the black street w/wild lies

❖

THE BLUES

O how could this be done to me
great dancer's Witness
God, you are a satyr in disguise
Thus cruelly & uselessly to
Rend my life awry
I'll lie here stolen, in cold wind
in the road, until peace freezes
                              over,
& hallows me.
Rude ghost bastard.
Ah! Who comes now.

❖

AN AFTERNOON OF SUMMER

an afternoon of summer
              dread
I'm afraid to meet all
        the rest of my brothers
        in distress
Couldn't we get in one
        big Movie
Blow it all on one
        Grand Floozie
           & end it all
             YAH
             YEAH
an autograph sends respects
        to her Twin

everyone wants a Christ
        & no one will give it to him
Mohammed, the enchanter
           Keeper of Harems

Buddha, inkindergardened
        under his tree, w/
not a moon-glow,
      mindless Thought for you
          & me

AN AFTERNOON OF SUMMER

(This does not mean I want
    or wish to be prey to people
            God forbid)

            & look at the steeple
a mindless wit am I
dickless, looking at the sky

❖

A HOLE IN THE CLOUDS

a hole in the clouds
where a mind hides
Pagodas—temples

in child's raw hope

animal in a tunnel
defined by the light
around him

These evil subsidies
these shrouds
surround

❖

IF IT'S NO PROBLEM...

If it's no problem, why mention it.
Everything spoken means that,
it's opposite, & everything else.
I'm alive, I'm dying.

❖

THE END OF THE RAINBOW

The end of the rainbow

put all my screaming phantasies
into one giant
Box-trap

image of self-image-propagation
image of elation

Ungulation
limit 1st tree

image of Utopia
a slaughter of phantoms

innocent—guilty

The Human World
bounded by words
& dust

sweet soft & velvet
dust

medium trust

❖

HEAVEN OR HELL...

Heaven or Hell the circus
of your actions

To Play
(chance is god here)
at Carnival

assuage the guilt
The deep fear

The separate loneliness

open Sinygog
open sesame

The Party of new connections
mind made free
Love cannot save you
from your own fate

Art cannot soothe
Words cannot tame
The Night

❖

SCOUR THE MIND...

Scour the mind w/diamond
brushes. Cleanse into Mandalas.
Memory keeps us wicked & warm.
The Time temple. Who'll go 1st?
Cloaked figures huddled by walls.
A head moves clocklike slowly.
I'm coming. Wait for me.

❖

Lessons on becoming
    a revolutionary
    an actor
        (a phrophet!)
    or a poet
There's still good friends
    to assist & relieve you
    mercenary whim
    for her or for him

First become a
    visionary-scientist
    radical biochemical
    aviationary sky-diver
Then contact your local pub-
lic accountant (he'll tell you
how to spread the seeds of doubt)

LESSONS ON BECOMING

Lessons on becoming
    a revolutionary
    an actor
      (a prophet!)
    or a poet

There's still good friends
    to assist & relieve you
    Mercenary whim
    for her or for him

First become a
    Visionary-Scientist
    radiocal biochemical
    aviationary sky-diver
Then contact your local pub-
lic accountant (he'll tell you
how to spread the seeds of doubt)

❖

MAIDS ARE BICKERING...

Maids are bickering in the hall
The day is warm
Last night's perfume
I lie alone in this
cool room

My mind is calm & swirling
like the marble pages of an
old book

I'm a cold clean skeleton
scarecrow on a hill
in April
Wind eases the arches
of my boney Kingdom
Wind whistles thru my mind
& soul
My life is an open book
or a T.V. confession

❖

HURRICANE & ECLIPSE

I wish a storm would
come & blow this shit
away. Or a bomb to
burn the Town & scour
the sea. I wish clean
death would come to me.

❖

If only I
could Feel
The Sound
    of the sparrows
I Feel Child hood
pulling me
    back again

If only I could Feel
me pulling back
        again
I Feel embraced
by reality
        again

    I would die (Be)
~~would~~ Gladly die

IF ONLY I

If only I
       could feel
The sound
       of the sparrows
& feel child hood
       pulling me
            back again

If only I could feel
       me pulling back
            again
& feel embraced
       by reality
            again
I would die
       Gladly die

❖

IT HAS BEEN SAID...

It has been said that
on birth we are trying
to find a proper womb
for the growth of our
Buddha nature, & that
on dying we find a
womb in the tomb of the
earth. This is my
father's greatest
fear. It shouldn't be.
Instead, he should
be trying to find me
a better tomb.

❖

THE END OF THE DREAM

The end of the dream
will be when it
matters

all things lie
Buddha will forgive me
Buddha will

❖

AUGMENT OF RE-BIRTH

—The cycle begins anew

a luring lulling sick-sad maddening
   haunting ego-familiar strain
   calls the wayward wanderer
      home again

a music mosaic made of all image
   tunes preceding   ·

The whistle or warm woman's cry that
   calls the child home from play

❖

THANK YOU, O LORD

Thank you, O Lord
For the white blind light
A city rises from the sea
I had a splitting headache
from which the future's made.

❖

❖

PARIS JOURNAL

So much forgetten already
So much forgotten
So much to forget

Once the idea of purity
born, all was lost
irrevocably

The Black Musician
in a house up the hill

Nigger in the woodpile
Skeleton in the closet

Sorry. Didn't mean you.

An old man, someone's
                    daughter

Arises
& sees us still in the room
of off-key piano & bad
paintings

him off to work
& new wife arriving

(The candle-forests of
Notre-Dame)

beggar nuns w/moving
smiles, small velvet sacks
& cataleptic eyes

straying to the gaudy
Mosaic calendar
Windows

I write like this
  to seize you

give me your love, your
tired eyes, sad for
delivery

A small & undiscover'd
park—we ramble

And the posters scream
safe revolt

& the tired walls barely
fall, graffiti into
dry cement sand

an overfed vacuum
dust-clock

I remember freeways

Summer, beside you
Ocean—brother

Storms passing

electric fires in the night

"rain, night, misery—
the back-ends of wagons"

Shake it! Wanda,
fat stranded swamp
Woman

We still need you

Shake your roly-poly
Thighs inside that
Southern tent

So what.

It was really wild
She started nude & put
on her clothes.

An old & cheap hotel
w/bums in the lobby
genteel bums of satisfied
poverty

Across the street, a
famous pool-hall
where the actors meet

former ace—home of
beat musicians
beat poets & beat
wanderers

in the Zen tradition
from China to the
Subway
          in 4 easy lifetimes

Weeping, he left his pad
on orders from police
& furnishings hauled
away, all records &
momentos, & reporters
calculating tears &
curses for the press:

"I hope the Chinese junkies
          get you"

& they will
for the poppy
rules the world

That handsome gentle
flower

Sweet Billy!

Do you remember
the snake
your lover

tender in the tumbled
brush-weed
sand & cactus

I do.

And I remember
Stars in the shotgun
night

eating pussy
til the mind runs
clean

Is it rolling, God

in the Persian Night?

"There's a palace
   in the canyon
   where you & I
   were born

   Now I'm a lonely Man
   Let me back into
   the Garden

   Blue Shadows
   of the Canyon
   I met you
   & now you're gone

   & now my dream is gone
   Let me back into your Garden

   A man searching
   for lost Paradise
   Can seem a fool
   to those who never
   sought the other world

   Where friends do lie & drift
   Insanely in
   Their own private gardens"

The cunt bloomed
& the paper walls
Trembled

A monster arrived
in the mirror
To mock the room
& its fool
alone

Give me songs
to sing
& emerald dreams
to dream

& I'll give you love
unfolding

Sun

underwater, it was
immediately strange
& familiar

the black boy's
from the boat, fins & mask,

Nostrils bled liquid
crystal blood
as they rose to surface

Rose & moved strong
in their wet world

Below was a Kingdom
Empire of still sand
& yes, party-colored
fishes
  —they are the last
            to leave
The gay sea

I eat you
avoiding your wordy
bones

& spit out pearls

The little girl gave
little cries of surprise
as the club struck
her sides

I was there
By the fire in the
Phonebooth

I saw them charge
& heard the indian
war-scream

felt the adrenalin
of flight-fear

the exhilaration of terror
sloshed drunk in
the flashy battle blood

Naked we come
& bruised we go
nude pastry
for the slow soft worms
below

This is my poem
for you
Great flowing funky flower'd beast

Great perfumed wreck of hell

Great good disease
& summer plague

Great god-damned shit-ass
Mother-fucking freak

You lie, you cheat,
you steal, you kill

you drink the Southern
Madness swill
of greed

you die utterly & alone

Mud up to your braces
Someone new in your
knickers

& who would that be?

You know

You know more
than you let on

Much more than you betray

Great slimy angel-whore
you've been good to me

You really have

been swell to me

Tell them you came & saw
& look'd into my eyes
& saw the shadow
of the guard receding
Thoughts in time
& out of season
The Hitchiker stood
by the side of the road
& levelled his thumb
in the calm calculus
of reason.

❖

NOTES

Preparing the Material for Publication

The American Night is the second volume of Morrison's poetry and writings posthumously published by Villard Books, and it completes the endeavor begun with the publication of *Wilderness* in 1988. The aim has been to release, in its best and most finished form, all of the author's writings. The material contained in these books comes, for the most part, from the journals, notebooks, typescripts and loose hand-written pages that Morrison left in the care of his wife, Pamela, at the time of his death in Paris in 1971.

While preparing *Wilderness* and *The American Night* for publication, we set two rules for ourselves: first, don't change anything, present the material exactly as it exists with all the faults and blemishes intact; second, trust the poet. Trust in the poet's genius and judgment, his craft and intelligence.

Frequently abstract, often layered with metaphors, similes and symbols, sometimes lacking apparent connective tissue, Jim's poetry confronted us with bold images and textures that were unwilling to reveal their meaning to a casual reading. When a poem was obscure, we had to trust that the poet had purposefully made the shell hard to crack. To gain entry we would need to leave behind our preconceived notions of what a poem should be and open ourselves to what these poems were: bold, unconventional, experimental, difficult and startling.

Notes on the Contents of *The American Night*

"An American Prayer"

This is one of Morrison's major works. He read these poems in public on several occasions, and recorded them in 1970. The opening poem was self-published as a small book, which he gave to friends. This is the first publication of the entire work.

Tape Noon

A collection of finished drafts of poems, from several notebook sources that were gathered by the poet under this title in a single notebook. Although the meaning of the title remains a mystery, these poems were intended to be published together.

"Celebration of the Lizard"

A performance piece composed for the rock stage whose elements include songs, poetry, sound effects, music and, to a certain degree, audience participation.

From the evidence in his notebooks, Jim was thinking about and writing portions of "Celebration" as early as the summer of 1965. Over the next three years it was written and rewritten, dozens of times.

A printed version of the work appears on the inside cover of the Doors third album, *Waiting for the Sun,* released in 1968. The Doors recorded the piece and released it on the record, *Absolutely Live.*

"The Soft Parade"

Another theater piece, again composed of spoken and sung

portions, with room for other elements that Morrison, the performer, could add improvisationally. A recording of "The Soft Parade" is included on the Doors album of the same name.

Poems from The Village Reading

Included in this section are poems that Morrison recorded at Village Recorders in Los Angeles, the evening of December 8, 1970. We can trace the origin of each of these poems to one of his notebooks; and many of the works may have been written as early as 1964.

A record album of the poetry was assembled and released in 1978. In 1979, this album, *An American Prayer,* was nominated for a Grammy in the spoken word category. Included on the recording is the first half of the poem "An American Prayer."

"The Hitchhiker"

Dated 1969, "THE HITCHHIKER, An American Pastoral" is a screenplay treatment combining dialogue with dramatic action that was to have been the basis for a motion picture script. Several scenes were filmed and assembled (under the title "HWY") in an effort to raise funds to complete the project.

"Dry Water"

A single book-length work consisting of a series of shorter poems. Several portions have been published in *Wilderness* and together with the poems published here they constitute the entire work. A selection of the poems was published in the Los Angeles *Image* in October 1969. And in January

1971 *Circus* magazine published three other poems from the work.

Lyric Verse

Jim Morrison wrote more than 100 songs, in a variety of musical styles: blues, sea chanteys, ballads and rock. One song, "Woman in the Window," is based on a melody by Johann Sebastian Bach.

Notebook Poems

A selection of finished poems and aphorisms from Morrison's notebooks, journals and loose handwritten pages. Almost all the poems printed here were composed during the period 1965 to 1971.

"Paris Journal"

The entire notebook consists of one angry, reflective and defiant poem. As there are only three places in the notebook where words or phrases have been crossed out, this appears to be a clean and finished draft. He wrote the title, "Paris Journal," on the front of the notebook's black cover, and at the end of the notebook he appended his personal image/symbol: the hitchhiker, alone, by the side of the open road. These were among the last lines he wrote.

Columbus B. Courson   Frank Lisciandro
Pearl Marie Courson   Katherine Lisciandro

INDEX of FIRST LINES